dealing with
EATING DISORDERS

Kate Haycock

Wayland

Bullying

Eating Disorders

Relationships

Substance Abuse

Death

Family Break-up

Editor: Deb Elliott

Concept design: Joyce Chester

Book design: Helen White

First published in 1994 by Wayland

(Publishers) Ltd

61 Western Road, Hove,

East Sussex BN3 1JD

British Library Cataloguing in Publication

Data

Haycock, Kate

  Eating Disorders. - (Dealing With Series)

  I. Title II. Series

  616.85

ISBN 0 7502 0989 5

Typeset by White Design

Printed and bound by Canale in Italy

All of the people who appear in the
photographs in this book are models.

Contents

What are eating disorders?

▶ **'Come on sweetheart. Just one more mouthful for daddy. It's good for you.'**

From about the age of three months, when babies are introduced to the world of 'solids', or real food, the kitchen table can become a battlefield and food can become a weapon. How many desperate parents have been heard to promise that if you eat up your greens, you can have some sweets? From infancy, through childhood, adolescence and then adulthood, we realise the importance of food. It is not just a source of life or a necessity for good health, it can also be a powerful bargaining tool. However, seeing it as such can lead to misery, depression, and life-threatening situations.

There are many reasons why people develop eating disorders. There are also a number of different eating disorders. The common factor is emotional pain.

When Karen Carpenter, the singer with the pop group, The Carpenters, died in 1983, the news shocked the world. She had died of anorexia nervosa, an illness in which the sufferer stops eating to the point of starvation.

Karen Carpenter was from a close-knit, upper middle-class American family. She had always been influenced strongly by her parents throughout her life. So much so, in fact, that when she left home finally, at the age of twenty-six, she moved into an apartment only a very short distance from her parents' home.

An eating disorder is the name given to problems relating to people's eating patterns. Whether they are due to eating too much or too little, they cause serious distress to those affected. Many of these problems can be avoided, however, and many can be cured if they are treated in the early stages.

We regulate our food intake naturally by responding to our body's needs - when we are hungry, we eat, when we are full, we stop eating. Each of us is different.

Karen worked with her brother, Richard, who had very high standards which she tried hard to meet. In short, her whole life was spent trying to live up to the demands and expectations of other people.

Karen Carpenter developed anorexia. Over a period of ten years, the singer wasted away, slowly and painfully, although the public and her adoring fans never knew. Indeed, when her death was first reported, it was stated that she had died of a sudden heart attack and had been in good health. Ultimately, her death was caused by a heart attack, but it was a heart weakened by starvation.

Anorexia is one of the most extreme forms of eating disorders.

▲ **Karen Carpenter's life ended tragically in 1983, when she lost her battle against anorexia nervosa.**

▼ **The common factor in all eating disorders is that sufferers are in emotional distress.**

Each of us needs different quantities of food to be fit and healthy. People whose natural instincts and biological mechanisms do not reliably tell them how much to eat or not eat are considered to have eating disorders.

Eating disorders come in several different forms. Anorexia nervosa literally means a nervous loss of appetite, although it was given this name a long time ago when the disease was not wholly understood. In fact, someone suffering from anorexia has not lost his or her appetite, but controls and drastically reduces the amount of food eaten, to the point of starvation. The cause is often seen as a desire to be slim, hence the nickname 'the slimmers' disease', but the root of the disorder goes much deeper and is often due to a variety of psychological problems. In its most severe form, as in Karen Carpenter's case, it can be fatal.

Bulimia nervosa is a condition related to anorexia. Bulimia sufferers, or bulimics, are unable to control their weight through the amount they eat.

◀ Anorexia is often seen as the 'slimmers' disease' — a diet that has gone too far. However, the true cause of the disease is often due to psychological problems.

The pattern for bulimics is to eat vast quantities of food in one go, and then make themselves throw up what they have eaten.

Compulsive eating is when someone eats abnormally large amounts of food out of habit or due to anxiety. For example, someone who 'comfort eats' during a crisis or personal problem. Some of the sufferers are obese or bulimics, but even when it does not reach such serious proportions, compulsive eating is a disorder which causes the sufferer much distress.

▼ Obesity, or the state of being grossly overweight, can be due to a medical problem, but is usually the result of an eating disorder - not being able to control the amount one eats and eating too much.

Understanding anorexia

Sophie had a happy home life. Her family had a lovely house, and Sophie was popular, successful at school and good at sport. She was keen on acting and, at the age of fifteen, she auditioned for a part in the school play. Someone told her she wouldn't get the part because the character in the play needed to be played by a very thin person.

Sophie had really wanted the part and, although she was not overweight, she decided to go on a diet.

37.8 kilogrammes (6 stones), that they decided she should see a doctor. She was diagnosed as anorexic.

Sophie is a typical anorexic in many ways. She had a secure family background, and seemed to excel in everything she did. She was very competitive, and liked to come top in exams. Her parents encouraged her always to do her best.

It was only when she detected a chink in her ability to shine, namely not getting the part she wanted in a play, that things changed. She was afraid of failure and worried that she may be letting her parents down. She decided to take control of herself and reduce weight.

Before too long, she was obsessed by her diet and losing weight, and hardly ate anything. Since starting her diet, Sophie had become much more of a loner. She spent a lot of time studying in her room, and no longer wanted to go to her friends' houses or parties. Instead of playing tennis, which she used to play very well, she started running long distances, almost every day. She would get up extra early before school to have time for her run.

Her parents tried to get her to eat, and became increasingly concerned that Sophie had lost her appetite. However, it was not until a year later, when Sophie's weight had fallen below

Many girls who become anorexic have never been rebellious. Their parents describe them as well-behaved children who have never caused any problems. In fact, Sophie's parents thought that she was such a clever girl, to whom everything always came naturally, and who never had any problems, that it took a long time for them to notice the extent to which she had stopped eating.

However, a comment like this may make a child feel that she has failed in some way if she is not really slim.

As children we are told to eat what we are given. Sometimes we are not allowed to leave the table until we have finished everything on our plates. If we do not eat, our parents get worked up because they are worried that we are not getting enough nutrition, or they are concerned about the waste of perfectly good food. We soon learn that if we do not eat, we will become the focus of our parents' attention.

◀ **Society places a great value on 'being slim'. This encourages women to diet and 'weight watch'. Unfortunately, parents who allow themselves to become obsessed with diets and** **losing weight can pass this anxiety on to their children.**

▼ **Many children go through a phase of 'fussy eating', but they develop a sensible attitude to food.**

Why do people stop eating?

Teenagers, especially girls, tend to worry about their weight, although very few are overweight. Anorexia, however, does not necessarily start with a desire to lose weight. People stop eating for much more complex reasons. Some of these derive from the relationship with food which we develop when we are very young.

Parents can easily pass on their own concerns about their weight and what they eat. A mother who makes a great effort to 'keep her figure' may think she is being helpful when she says to her daughter, 'If you start watching your figure now, it'll be easier when you get older.'

Some still crave attention from their mother, father or other adults, and continue to use food as a way of getting noticed.

The need for attention can be triggered off by many things. Parents who argue constantly or who are in the process of a divorce may cause a child to feel unloved. A troublesome sister or brother may occupy all the parents' time, leaving the 'trouble-free' child feeling ignored. A death or tragedy in the family may divert a parent's attention, and again the child may feel unnoticed.

Parents may exert pressure on their children to succeed at school, or to be good at sports.

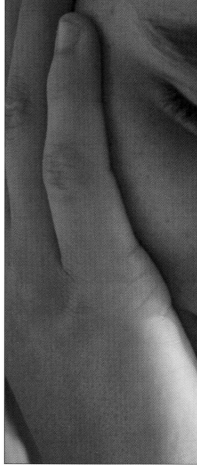

▲ **Many young people try very hard to please their parents, and to live up to or even exceed their expectations. Sometimes they try too hard and this leads to pressure and stress.**

◄ **Teenage years are often described as 'the best years of your life'. However, teenage years can be beset with problems and pressures. The pressure to do well at school and pass exams can be very hard to handle.**

Initially it is very hard to stop eating, but after a while anorexics get a thrill from denying themselves food. They may become obsessed by the weight they are losing, or with the small amount of food they can 'survive' on. Or they will feel satisfied that, although they have no control over their parents' arguments, or their failure at school, they have managed to control their food intake, which they see as a victory.

Being slim and able to control the amount you eat is admired in our society, so the person denying him or herself food is often envied, which spurs him or her on to continue the starvation diet. It is not uncommon to hear teenage girls say of an anorexic classmate, 'I wish I could catch that for a while'. They do not realise that the sufferer is desperately unhappy, and would give anything to be 'normal' like her friends.

What does it feel like to be an anorexic?

It is very difficult to persuade anorexics to describe honestly how they feel. They are often very secretive, and are afraid to lose control by speaking about their feelings and worries. Many anorexics do, however, keep diaries which reveal their true feelings.

This does not take into account the child's own inclinations and interests. Young boys may feel they cannot or do not want to fulfil a parent's desire for them to be a good footballer or athlete. In desperation to have their needs noticed, a young person may use the only way he or she knows - to stop eating.

Another reason why people may stop eating stems from the pressure on them to be 'perfect'. As in Karen Carpenter's case, people in the public eye are particularly susceptible to the pressure to be slim. Actors, celebrities and members of the royal family are worshipped. Much is expected of them and they strive to fulfil what they believe to be society's expectations of them.

Anorexia is also agonizingly common among people whose job is to be fit, slim and beautiful, such as models, athletes and ballet dancers. They become so obsessed with the need to be a certain shape for their career, that they develop a distorted relationship with food.

Parveen kept a diary during the four years that she was ill with anorexia. Parveen weighed herself every day when she got up. This was one of the most important events in her day. If her weight had gone up slightly, she would be depressed. She would then make sure she ate less during that day. Often these weight increases would be only a few grammes.

If her weight was less or stable, this would please her and encourage her to

'I am always cold, and my hair is falling out. I don't like to sit down for very long as it really hurts because I don't have enough flesh. I have nothing in common with my friends. I feel really alone.'

Occasionally, she would acknowledge the fact that she should put on weight for her health's sake. *'I know that I must put on weight, but I am so terrified of doing this. I wish I could look and feel like other girls my age.'*

continue her minuscule diet. At one stage she ate only an apple and an egg daily. If she 'slipped up' and ate more, whether it be a salad, a cracker or an extra drink, she would be filled with fear about what her weight would be the next day, and would be even more harsh with herself about what she could eat.

Parveen filled the day before and after school with homework, housework and vigorous exercise. She would walk to school and back, and would go for long walks and do aerobic exercises when she came home. Often she would be cleaning the house until late at night. If she ate more than she had intended to, she would do extra exercise to burn off the calories.

Many times in Parveen's diary, she talks about how she feels.

These feelings would not last very long, however, and panic would rise as soon as her weight went up by another few grammes.

Parveen criticized herself constantly for what she was doing to her family. *'I feel so awful for being like this. I know it is making everyone unhappy. They* (her parents) *are so good to me, so patient and supportive, but I feel trapped. Deep down I seriously don't think that I can ever put on weight. I can't imagine eating normally and swallowing again. I feel such a burden to my family and friends.'*

As Parveen became weaker, even little things became more of an effort: getting up, cleaning her room, going to school. But she drove herself on. In the diary she describes how she found it impossible to concentrate at times.

Parveen's diary shows what a miserable affliction anorexia is. The sufferer feels unhappy, confused, isolated and alone. He or she is often aware of the problems but is powerless to help him or herself. The anorexic is obsessed with food, and is hungry to the point of starvation, but is somehow unable to eat more than the odd morsel.

While others can see the effects of the disease on his or her emaciated body, the sufferer is unable to see anything but fat and, as a result, is forced to diet more and more harshly.

If an anorexic does not eat, the body's faculties become weakened. Hormones become disrupted. Girls' periods stop (a condition called amenorrhoea). Often they do not return for a long time after the patient is cured.

Boys who develop anorexia have usually not yet been through puberty, and the process of puberty will stop until they have recovered. Anorexics suffer tooth and hair loss, and fine hair often grows over the body and face.

Damage to the kidneys is very common. The effects of long-term starvation can be fatal, although anorexics are incredibly robust and can survive at extremely low weights for a long time.

One of the most upsetting aspects of anorexia is the effect that the sufferer's behaviour has on his or her family. Often the anorexic controls what the family eats, too.

◄ **It can take a long time for the symptoms of anorexia to become obvious. A sufferer can appear to have lost weight, and may seem rather depressed. The serious physical effects may take a while before anyone notices that something is wrong.**

One parent describes her son: *'Giles became obsessed with cooking and preparing rich and elaborate foods for us. He would insist that we ate everything, and would watch us while we did, but would not eat himself.*

'In one phase, he would get up early and cook pastries and cakes, and would not let the other children go to school until everything had been eaten.

'He also had special routines, such as family mealtimes, and if anyone was late, or there was an unexpected delay, he became hysterical. We found it difficult to refuse his demands, for fear of upsetting him further, and this caused an immense strain on the other children.'

Anorexics who eventually become cured speak of the awful waste of their lives during the time they were ill. They feel guilty about the strain it had on their families and other relationships.

Anyone suffering from anorexia at any stage needs and must seek help. In Chapter 6 we will look at the types of treatment available, and in Chapter 7 there is advice for anyone who is concerned that they may be developing an eating disorder.

▼ There is no doubt about it, anorexia is a wretched illness, and one which the sufferers would give anything not to have.

▶ Family mealtimes can be very stressful for an anorexic. They become a focal point for his or her obsession with food.

Compulsive eating, bulimia and obesity

While anorexia is the most visible, distressing and life-threatening of eating disorders, these other three conditions are common and are the cause of much misery for the sufferers.

At some time in our lives, we have all eaten because we were bored, fed up or lonely. It is often said that food is a substitute for love. A compulsive eater, though, is someone who eats regularly to fill emptiness or boredom. They have an obsession with food, talking about it, thinking about it and preparing it during most of their waking hours.

Compulsive eating is very common among women. It develops in women with a poor self-image, who feel they are overweight, or because someone else, possibly a husband or boyfriend, has made them feel uncomfortable about their body.

Although the compulsive eater may appear normal and cheerful, she is often secretly very unhappy. She may live with a compulsive eating disorder for many years, or even her whole life.

Andrea is a compulsive eater.

'I sometimes wake up in the middle of the night and crave food. I go into the kitchen and go through the refrigerator, eating any leftovers. Then I start on the dried foods - I will eat dry spaghetti out of the packet, raisins, oats, anything. I feel a need in my mouth. I just want to fill it with food.

'When I binge, I do not enjoy the food I am eating. Often I don't even taste it. I just have to eat something.

'Afterwards, I feel disgusted with myself. I want to hide away from the world, so I just curl up on the sofa and go to sleep.'

▲ Compulsive eaters are unhappy with their body shape. They have a 'fear of food' and regularly go on diets. They lose some weight, but then something will happen which will upset their routine, and they will start bingeing again.

Bulimia

Compulsive eating has much in common, both in its causes and in the obsession with food, with the more serious condition known as bulimia. The word 'bulimia' literally means 'having an appetite like an ox'. It is used to describe the eating disorder of someone who eats huge amounts, usually in a very short space of time, and then forces herself (sufferers are usually female) to vomit.

As bulimics are, generally, very secretive, and because they seem to stay at a fairly steady weight, their condition does not tend to be noticed as easily as anorexia.

Bulimia does not necessarily develop from anorexia, although Gloria's tale (see opposite) is typical of the way the two conditions cross over. In many ways, someone with bulimia is much closer to a compulsive eater. They both have a poor self-image and the same distorted relationship with food. At times it is a source of comfort, but it is also an enemy. Bulimics eat despite feeling that they should not. They feel guilty, so that the act of vomiting is like a form of punishment.

Although a bulimic will not starve to death, self-induced vomiting is dangerous. Vomit is very acidic, and will, after a period of time, erode the enamel on the teeth, causing tooth decay. In severe cases, vomiting can lead to dehydration and the loss of important minerals, causing weakness and cramps.

From putting two fingers down their throats, bulimics will often have scars or calluses on their fingers. Their faces may have a puffy appearance, with burst blood vessels. Sufferers are usually extremely unhappy, are obsessed with food and have a fear of putting on weight.

Mara was a bulimic for four years. She describes how she felt when she had the disease.

'I hated myself. I felt really fat, although I realise now I was not.

'At the beginning I thought everything would be all right if I could lose weight, but then I just became miserable and apathetic. I had no interest in anything any more. I felt unpopular, depressed, alone. The vomiting was like a punishment to my body for being so ugly. I was so desperate at times that I considered committing suicide. I just felt I had nothing to live for.'

Gloria developed bulimia after being treated in hospital for anorexia.

'In hospital, I was forced to eat, although I didn't want to. The nurses would not let me get out of bed, have visitors or anything unless I ate. They told me that this would carry on until I reached the target weight they had set for me. After a while I gave in. They weighed me weekly, and I soon learned to stuff myself before the weigh-in, so that I could have more freedom. Finally they were satisfied with the amount of weight I had put on, and let me leave hospital.

'The problem was, I had started to get used to eating, but I really hated my body now it was fat again. So I tried making myself sick after eating, and found out that I could bring up most of the food that I'd swallowed! It seemed like a miracle. Not only could I eat what I wanted, but I could stop myself from putting on weight.

'I carried on vomiting in secret. No one guessed, and my family were really pleased at how I had regained a normal appetite. Everyone kept saying how good I looked, but I felt really fat. So I stopped eating for a few weeks to lose some weight, and then I started eating and vomiting again.

'I then tried laxatives as well as vomiting, and found I could keep my weight down pretty well, even after the huge amounts I ate. On a 'binge' I would cram into my mouth cream cakes, cereal, toast, cheese, fruit, ice-cream, chocolate bars, sausages, cold food from the refrigerator, anything I could find. Of course a lot of this I had to do in secret, either when the family were out, or I would sneak food into my room a bit at a time, hide it under the bed and then eat it late at night. Then I would go into the bathroom and throw it all up. I was taking about fifty laxatives a day at my worst.'

Obesity

Walter Hudson was an American man who died recently weighing 535.5 kilogrammes (about 85 stones). He was obese. He spent his entire day eating. He could not get out of bed, so his whole family had to shop for him and bring him his food. When he died, his body had to be cut out of his flat by fire fighters.

Walter Hudson may have been an extreme case, but there are many people who are obese.

▲ **The American Walter Hudson, who weighed 535.5 kilogrammes.**

eople who eat too much and ecome obese also frequently ave the problems of low self-steem which are related to the ther eating disorders.

Corinne was 88 kilogrammes (14 stones) when her doctor told her she was obese. Rather than have the desired effect of making her lose weight, his comments made her feel so miserable that she ate more than ever, became extremely depressed and put on 37.8 kilogrammes (6 stones) in the next six months. She had no confidence and hated leaving the house.

▼ **In recent years, doctors have focused on obesity as a cause of many illnesses and health problems, such as high blood pressure and heart attacks.**

Although obesity can be serious, it is important to realise that being slightly overweight is not the same as being obese. Because of the way fat people are sometimes treated by society, many of us have a fear of being obese, and worry about a little bit of extra flesh.

As a teenager, it is extremely unlikely that you are in fact obese. If you feel that you are overweight, ask for a second opinion and see a sympathetic doctor. Try to be a bit more careful about what you eat and do more exercise. If you feel that your problem is due to your poor self-image, you may find it useful to read Chapter 8.

Who gets eating disorders?

Many of the most serious eating disorders tend to affect teenagers and people in their early twenties. By far the majority are female.

So why teenagers? For a start, a lot happens when you're a teenager. First of all, your body changes. You go through puberty. As a result of hormones, you start feeling different, and you start looking different. Boys develop facial hair and their voices deepen. Girls develop breasts and start menstruating. Their bodies become more curvaceous as they

◀▲ Puberty can be a difficult time for teenagers. It is a time of change, both physically and emotionally.

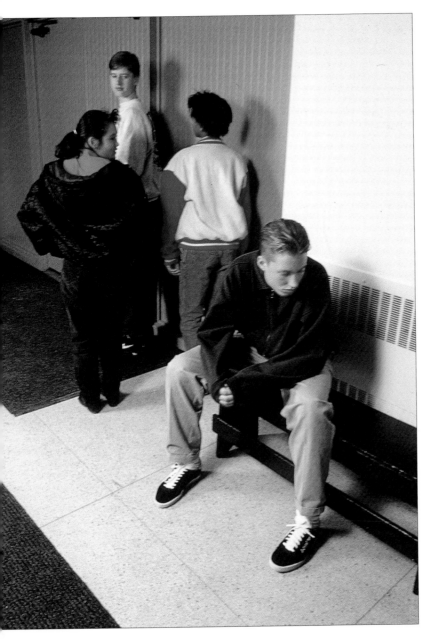

◀ The need to 'belong', to be part of a group or gang, can cause teenagers to behave differently. Some may start smoking or drinking, just so they will be accepted by their peers.

you. You feel like an adult but also feel that they still treat you like a child.

You become a lot more aware about what's going on in the world. You may be depressed or anxious about politics, the environment, war or nuclear power, and you feel powerless to do anything.

You are going out and meeting different people with new ideas and attitudes, and you suddenly start questioning your life, your upbringing and all the values you had taken for granted until now.

There is peer pressure to smoke, try drugs, dye your hair, pierce your ears or nose, and be part of a group.

In addition to all this you have the pressure of exams and choosing subjects and a career. It's hardly surprising that few of us sail through our adolescence. What happens is that we tend to

change from girls to women. Some girls are very self-conscious about these changes, particularly if they start earlier than their friends.

You start being interested in the opposite sex. You are given more freedom by your parents, but suddenly that freedom is not

enough. You want to experiment with different things, and often your parents want to stop you. They say that you can't go out looking like that or they won't let you stay out late. They complain about the music you play and they won't let you decorate your bedroom the way you want to. They don't seem to understand

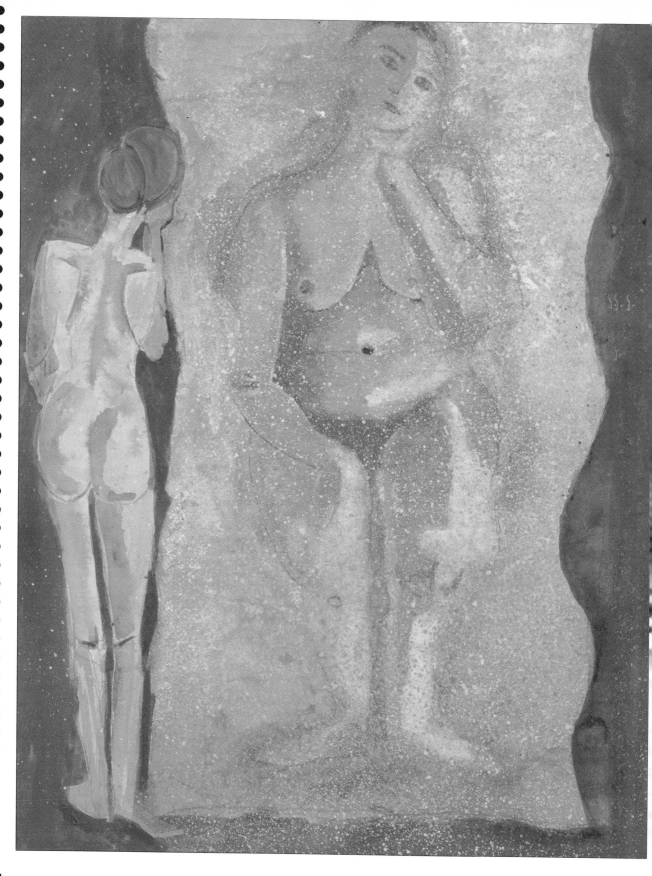

ave an identity crisis. We worry
bout who we are, whether we
re popular, and what we look
ke. These are problems related
o our self-image - how we see
urselves.

elf-image is central to the
roblems of eating disorders.
long with the rest of society,
nany young people feel that the
vay they look is important for
eing accepted and liked. They
eel that if they can look right,
verything else will be all right
oo. Being a certain size or weight
an thus very quickly become an
bsession. They see it as the key
o sorting out all the confusion
ney feel. This can lead to a
reoccupation with eating and
ood.

lthough there are people of both
exes with eating disorders, most
norexics and bulimics are girls
or women. Many experts feel that
his is due to the extreme
ressure on women in our society
o be slim. But why have the last
wenty years seen a massive
ncrease in the number of cases?

◄ **This illustration is of
norexia nervosa. The basic
ause of the disease is
nknown. Mostly it affects
young women and girls, soon
after puberty.**

▲ **Many young people have a
very distorted picture of
themselves. They look in the
mirror and think they are
ugly, fat and spotty, when in
reality they look fine and are
no different to anyone else.**

Conflicting messages

▲ **Eating is an important social activity. Just sharing crisps and snacks can add to an evening's fun.**

Most of us have enough to eat. In our society, the sensation of true hunger is unfamiliar to most of us. When we have not eaten for a few hours, have been doing strenuous exercise, or when we get up in the morning, we may say 'I'm absolutely starving', but true starvation means serious deprivation of food over a long period of time.

We live in a society where there is more than enough food for everyone. Indeed, if we consider the easy availability of food, it's surprising that we aren't all extremely fat. Our society revolves around food. Eating out is a social activity - in restaurants, snack bars, pubs, coffee shops, tea shops, wine bars, or at dinner parties. Everywhere we go there is a place to buy food - corner shops, sandwich shops, supermarkets, late-night grocer's, chip shops, takeaways, and delicatessens.

Food is essential. We need it not only to be healthy but also to live. A nutritious and balanced diet is one of the best steps towards good health. But there is so much food to choose from. Advertisers, in their attempts to make us spend more money on their products, tempt and tantalize us with new concoctions. Their messages are very persuasive.

Mouth-watering images of cream cakes, ice-creams or exotic foods are all aimed at whetting our appetites and making us spend our money. By using clever slogans, we are encouraged to treat ourselves to something special, whether it be a chocolate bar or a pizza. The images of beautiful people, laughing, holding hands, running on the beach, are subliminal messages which suggest that by eating this food, we too will look like them or be like them.

We do not only eat when we are feeling hungry. We are easy to influence. We buy snacks - often tempted by the smell or the packaging. We eat because other people are eating or after seeing an advertisement for a new or

Fat people are often ridiculed. In school, fat children are teased, called names, are left out and are generally made to feel miserable.

tasty food. We eat because food is put in front of us. Many of us do not stop when we are full, but eat more than enough to satisfy our hunger. Often we will only stop because our plates are empty, or because we can not manage another mouthful.

So the media is responsible for trying to get us to eat more. But although we know that the more you eat, the fatter you get, when we look around at adverts we see

very few fat people advertising these products. In fact, the only times we see fat people used in food advertisements are for slimming products.

Fat people are often the butt of jokes. They are criticized for being unhealthy, lazy and greedy. They find it hard to buy fashionable clothes that fit, and are attacked by the medical profession which constantly tells them to lose weight.

In addition, they experience prejudice in job interviews, feel intimidated in communal changing rooms because of their size and spend their lives squeezing into seats made for 'average-sized' people.

This prevailing attitude towards fat people in society makes many very embarrassed by their size, and they frequently feel depressed and worthless because of it.

This has not always been the case. In many cultures today, where people still have to find their own food by hunting, farming or gathering, fatness is a symbol of beauty. Girls are fed huge quantities to make them attractive for marriage. Likewise, in ancient history, fat women were worshipped. They were seen as symbols of fertility. Artists throughout the ages, such as Rubens and Renoir, glorified large and voluptuous women.

◄ **Bather Sitting Drying her Leg. This painting by Pierre Auguste Renoir, found in the Museo De Arte in Sao Paulo, Brazil, shows the artist's view of larger women as symbols of beauty.**

Today, supermodels such as Naomi Campbell are famous because of their beauty and slim figures.

In the West, the opposite is now true. We have more than enough to eat, but it is slenderness that is attractive. Women who 'keep their figures' are admired, even if this involves a great deal of unhappiness and deprivation.

In the media, being slim, especially for women, is part of being attractive, successful, happy, popular, sexy, fashionable and in control of your life. We are bombarded on a daily basis with images of slim models and actresses.

When we open a magazine, we see features on how to achieve the perfect figure, or pages and pages of different 'wonder' diets. Diet books sell in their millions. Calories are counted on menus and on food packaging. We often go into clothes shops where the clothes are only made for a slim figure. New workout videos, featuring famous personalities, flood the market on almost a daily basis. Each one tells us how, like them, we can control our shape, and promises to give us their secret.

Is it any wonder that many of us feel a great desire to be slim, and get depressed when we think we are not?
It is very easy to become caught up in the hype of weighing ourselves daily, measuring ourselves, and talking about how much we weigh or how much we have or haven't eaten. We are careful to avoid too much fat, sugar, carbohydrate and cholesterol.

▼ **An artist's cartoon of society's fear of weight gain.**

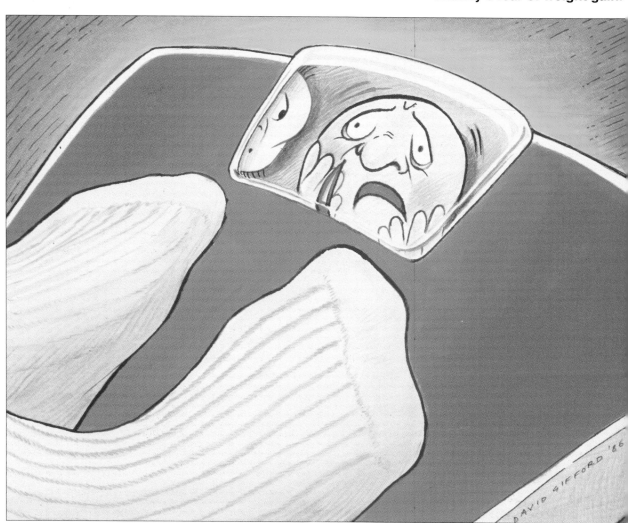

David was overweight, and he decided to go on a crash diet. He bought special 'meal-replacement' drinks from his chemist. Instead of eating a meal, he would have one of these drinks. Each drink contained 110 calories, giving him a daily intake of 330 calories. David formerly had been used to eating 5,000 calories or more.

Although he lost weight very quickly, he started having headaches and feeling nauseous and dizzy. He was extremely miserable, but he continued with the diet.

Eventually David decided to seek medical treatment for his headaches. According to his doctor, the headaches were a direct result of the diet.

The number of calories David was taking was far too small for his body. He was weak and unable to concentrate because he was simply not eating enough food. David's doctor gave him a much more sensible diet which meant he lost weight more slowly but more safely.

The lack of calories affected David's blood chemistry and blood sugar levels. Before long, he would have become dehydrated and constipated. Over a period of time, the body starves and starts to nourish itself on muscle. The heart is a muscle, and it is extremely dangerous if that is devoured in the body's attempts to continue all its functions. It will become weakened, bringing the person to the

Millions of people go on diets, many because they are influenced by society's message that if they can 'only shed that extra few kilogrammes', they will be more attractive, sexy, popular and successful. Although there is nothing wrong with sensible diets, problems begin when they get out of hand. Dieting can develop into anorexia, although there are other factors present. The obsession with losing weight is linked to bulimia and compulsive eating. Diets can work if they are controlled and gradual, but many crash diets and wonder diets can be extremely unsafe.

People can also experience a 'high' when they are on a very low-calorie diet, not unlike a 'high' from exercise or even from drugs. It can become addictive so they continue to diet for much longer than they should. Soon they can become very ill indeed.

Another problem with dieting is that when your body takes in less food than it needs, the body's reaction is to slow down and save energy. This reduces the metabolic rate. In other words, you are now burning fewer calories than you were before, so you will have to eat even fewer calories to lose weight.

Finally, a crash diet, or any diet, may work in the short term, but, in the long term, 98 per cent of all successful dieters go back to their former weight, and many actually increase their weight. The 'slimmers of the year', who drastically and rapidly reduce their weight and then put it all on again, place an enormous strain on their hearts, particularly if they go through this cycle several times. This can be more dangerous to health than the risks associated with being overweight.

All this means you should think very carefully about going on a diet, especially a crash diet. You need to ask yourself why you are so desperate to lose weight. Do you think it will change your life, or is there some other way?

In our daily lives, we receive two totally conflicting messages. On the one hand we are being tempted to eat and spend more, on the other we are pressurized to strive for physical 'perfection' as it is currently perceived. Societies that do not place a great value on thinness rarely have problems with eating disorders. Many experts agree that the pressure on people to be slim has contributed to an increase in eating disorders.

▼ The pressure on women, in particular, to be slim can lead to a distorted view of their body image.

What can be done about eating disorders?

Treating someone with an eating disorder is a very difficult task. A sufferer can be cured, but the earlier they are treated the better.

The first problem is recognizing that there is a problem. Anorexia, for example, often goes unnoticed for some time, as it is not abnormal for teenage girls to be conscious of their weight.

Daughters may assure their parents that they ate a lot at school, and that is why they are not hungry in the evening.

Parents do not notice how thin their child has become until, for example, they see a photo taken some time before, or the girl goes away for a few days, and they notice the difference on her return.

▲ **Parents often fail to recognize the signs of anorexia. They may think that their son or daughter is being more moody than usual, or is having a bad time at school.**

norexia is the most life-
hreatening of eating disorders. It
s very hard to force someone to
at - that is why not eating is a
ery effective form of protest or of
eeking attention. There comes a
tage in anorexia when the
ufferer is so ill that unless she
ats, she will die. At this stage,
he must go to hospital,
referably one which has a
pecialist ward for anorexics to
e nourished.

Many methods of nourishing
norexics have been tried over
he years. They may be force-fed,
r connected to a drip or have a
ube inserted down their throat,
nd confined to bed so that they
o not burn up any calories.
nother method is to encourage
he patient to eat by giving
rivileges if she eats, and
vithdrawing them if she does not.
rivileges include telephone calls,
isits, allowing her to write or
eceive letters, reading, or
vatching television.

◀▶ **Most of us have worries
bout our appearance at
ome time in our lives.
Anorexia is more than a
vorry about weight: it is a
ear. The disease affects
nainly teenage and young
idult women who may see
lieting as a way of
controlling their lives.**

Some specialist hospital wards
have communal dining areas,
where several anorexics eat
together. The idea here is peer
pressure: no one is allowed to
leave the table until everyone has
finished.

The problem with these
treatments is that, like Gloria, a
patient who does not want to put
on weight quickly learns it is
easiest to conform, so that she is
discharged as quickly as
possible.

Once she has left hospital, she rapidly loses the weight she has just gained. She will often become severely depressed by her new 'fat' body, and by her lack of control over her food intake. This has forced the medical profession to rethink its approach.

The main reason why none of the methods of 'feeding up' an anorexic are satisfactory is that they are only treating the symptom of the illness, not the cause. The act of not eating is not linked to loss of appetite, nor in most cases to the desire to be slim, but to psychological problems. Unless these are treated, the patient may survive, but the illness will not go away.

Treating the psychological aspects of the illness is a very specialized task. It often takes the form of therapy, where the trained therapist will develop a relationship with the sufferer and build up her confidence to discuss her childhood, her relationship with her parents and so on.

Often the parents will also be involved, as their relationship with the patient is often seen as a key factor in the development of the eating disorder. It is important that parents support and understand the treatment, so that they can continue to help while the patient

hopefully begins to recover. Some therapy involves the use of art and creative writing, which helps both the therapist and the patient to get to the root of the patient's problems.

When someone has anorexia or bulimia at an advanced stage, there will be many setbacks in the course of this treatment. It is a very slow and painful process and the therapist must have a lot of time and be extremely patient.

Changing the way you feel about your body, especially if you have other worries or problems, can seem impossible. A very effective way of coming to terms with an eating disorder is through self-help groups which exist all over the country. People get together in groups and talk about how they feel. Bulimics, compulsive eaters and people who overeat can all benefit. They learn that they are not alone, and get strength from the support of the others in the group. They talk about their problems, and start to understand why they developed their eating disorder.

Gloria is one of those who found a self-help group was very important for her to make a recovery.

'I was really lucky that I read about a self-help group which I started attending. It was such a

relief to find out that there were other people with the same problems. I honestly thought I was a freak. I felt so much better once I admitted that I binged and vomited. Everyone was so supportive, and after a very long, slow haul, I feel I am beginning now to put my bingeing days behind me. I don't think I'll ever feel totally safe around food again, though.'

Don't bottle it up!

Growing up is not easy, but everyone has to go through it. If anything is worrying you - your looks, your weight, your parents' relationship, your school work - the best thing you can do is talk to someone about it.

You may feel that you already have an eating disorder. First of all, if you are in any doubt at all, you must not ignore it. Any eating disorder, however slight it may seem now, is much easier to treat in the early stages.

▼ **Worries can easily get out of hand if you bottle them up. If you can get them off your chest, you will realise that you are not alone.**

It is important that you find someone as soon as possible who will listen to you and take you seriously. Whether you have a problem or not, the mere fact that you are worried means that you should be heard.

Talk to someone who you think will listen. It may be one or both of your parents, a sister or brother, an aunt, uncle or grandparent, older cousin or other relative. It may be a teacher, school nurse or counsellor. It may be your doctor, youth club leader, priest or vicar. It may be a friend's parent, brother or sister.

Tell them how you are feeling, and that you feel you need help. If they tell you not to worry so much, and you go away and are still worried, they are not the right person to talk to. Try again until you find someone who will take you seriously.

If talking just does not make you feel better, or you know that you have a problem with eating, then you need more help. Ask your confidante to help you find a doctor, or someone else qualified to help you. People involved in the organizations listed at the end of the book may be able to recommend where to go next.

Never think your problem is not important enough. Never think people around you are too busy to care or take you seriously. Try them. They may have been too busy to notice, but when they realise you have been storing up a big problem, they will often have time for you. Remember, if you become anorexic, or develop another serious eating disorder, everyone is going to be affected - your friends, your teachers, and most of all your family. Give them the chance to help you early on.

The world is a difficult place. No one can be expected to cope with it alone. Today there are experts for almost every problem or situation imaginable. If we want to buy a house, we seek the advice of a solicitor. If we want to have our hair cut, we go to a hairdresser. Similarly if we have problems with our friends, school or college work, boyfriends or girlfriends, or living with our parents, we need to talk about them, and gain from the experiences of others.

In the meantime, go to the library and find some books about what is worrying you. There are plenty of books on growing up, and being a teenager, and many on eating disorders, some of which are personal accounts from sufferers.

▶ **Sometimes talking is all you need. By confiding in a friend, you may find that they have similar worries. Then you can help each other.**

How to have a good self-image

Although being a teenager is often accompanied by the types of problems we looked at in Chapter 4, it is in actual fact a very exciting time. It is a time when we stop being children, and learn to become adults. All of a sudden we have new opportunities and freedoms. We have a chance to voice our opinions and be taken seriously. If we are positive, it can be one of the most challenging and rewarding times of our lives. So how do we make sure that we make the most of this time and don't waste the opportunities?

As we have seen, a poor self-image can be the root of many major problems. So how do we develop a good self-image?

Let's start with our bodies. For women to have children, they need a rounded shape. This is one of the changes that takes place when girls go through puberty. Very few women are intended to have rake-like bodies and flat stomachs. Such a shape has become fashionable, but only thirty years ago people considered Marilyn Monroe one of the most beautiful women ever and a symbol of the 'female' ideal. Monroe, however, had a

◄ Fashions change very quickly. In the late 1950s and early 1960s, actress Marilyn Monroe's curvy, size 16 figure was considered the height of fashion.

voluptuous, curvy body, and wore size 16 dresses! It just shows how quickly the 'ideal shape' can change.

When your body starts to change shape, it can often seem as if it is growing in an uneven way. This is perfectly normal, and it may take a little while before the changes all take place. In the meantime, your body needs energy to go through these changes, and for you to grow properly. For this reason, it is a very bad time to go on a diet. Try to wait a little longer, and then see how you feel about your shape when it has stopped changing. Then, if you are still unhappy, you may feel that you want to go on a diet, but with much less risk to your body growing properly.

◄ The mid to late 1960s saw Twiggy's waif-like size 8 figure take control of the fashion world. It is impossible for all women to be society's 'ideal shape'.

▲ **As a boy, you will probably have concerns about your body shape. Again, the most important thing that you can remember is that your body needs lots of energy to grow during adolescence. Try to leave it to its natural devices, eating normally and not exercising excessively until you have stopped growing.**

Take an interest in what is happening to your body and why. Get books out of the library which explain this fascinating process. Discuss it with your friends. Next time you are in a changing room in your favourite clothes shop, have a look at everyone else - you will see many different shapes and sizes and realise that there is no such thing as 'normal' or 'perfect'.

There are other aspects of our appearance which contribute to self-image - our skin, our hair, our clothes. Wash your hair regularly and go to the hairdresser's before it gets untidy. Keep your skin clean and brush your teeth.

People can be transformed just by these simple things. Even top models need a bit of help - a touch of make-up or a bit of hair gel, for example. If you feel pale, try getting out in the fresh air more. If you hate your glasses, consider contact lenses or ask for a new, trendier pair of glasses as a birthday present.

Don't just sit in your room moping - decide what you could improve and do something about it. Ask a good friend for advice - what would he or she change?

▼ The best way to be an interesting person is not by being thin and trendy, but by doing interesting things.

The clothes we wear tell people a lot about us. Interesting clothes are not necessarily the ones in all the magazines. Today there is more diversity and many more different 'looks' than ever before. Some styles only suit certain shapes. Don't be a slave to a fashion that doesn't suit your shape. Try to develop your own style. Don't just go to the high street shops. Try second hand stores, or go through your parents' or older brothers' and sisters' wardrobes. Pick up interesting bits of jewellery in jumble sales and junk shops.

Learn to make your own clothes - they're cheaper and you can get exactly what you want. Don't be a sheep - dare to be different.

If clothes don't fit you when you try them, don't buy them. We are all born different; the secret is to emphasize our good points. If you think you have nice legs, then wear clothes that show them off. If you are particularly proud of your broad shoulders, then accentuate them in your clothes.

If you feel that your life is far too ordinary, think about what you would most like to do, however unusual it is. Now, what's stopping you doing it?

You may want to go to Chile or Zimbabwe, so get involved with an organization like Raleigh

International which sets up expeditions to developing countries for people aged between seventeen and twenty-five. Even if you are still a few years too young, you could start planning for it now. Read about people who have been. What skills did they need? Are they

▼ **If you feel strongly about what's happening in the news or politics, get involved. Write to your MP or local newspaper. Join a campaigning organization or start a debating society at school.**

skills that you could be developing now?

Set yourself goals. If you love animals, get a pet, or if you can't, volunteer for work at a local animal sanctuary. Have you always wanted to be a song-writer? Speak to your music teacher at school for advice about how to learn more about song-writing.

Helping people is a good way of learning about other people's problems, and is enjoyable and satisfying. You get out of the house and into the real world and

will find that people treat you with the respect of an adult. How about visiting old people or walking a neighbour's dog?

If you are always short of money, consider ways of earning some. Washing cars, mowing lawns, babysitting or a part-time job when you're old enough are just some ideas.

Sport is one of the best ways to have a good time, meet other people, and keep fit at the same time. But don't limit yourself to school sports. If you fancy rowing there's probably a club near you

A healthy diet is important. Again, because your body is growing, don't skip meals, especially breakfast - even if you only have a bowl of cereal. Take an interest in the food you eat, and experiment with different foods. Try to eat a lot of fresh fruit and vegetables, pulses and wholemeal bread. If you don't like the food at school, take your own; it can then be as interesting as you want.

If you really feel that you do want to lose weight, try to find a way of doing it slowly and sensibly. Forget about crash diets and wonder pills. These are expensive and provide very little food value. The very best way to diet is to eat less of normal food, especially foods which are high in calories, such as cakes, pastries, chips, sausages and fried foods. You should also always increase the amount of exercise you do.

Remember society's obsession with weight, shape and fitness. Keep it in perspective. Sensible eating is the key. You don't have to give up anything - fizzy drinks, chocolate, hamburgers - as long as you try to have a balanced diet. We all need food, and we are lucky that we live in a society where there is more than enough to eat. Enjoy good food and you will benefit by feeling healthy and happy.

Exercise keeps your spirits up, and maintains or even increases your metabolic rate. As long as you don't overdo it, exercise is good for you.

which teaches people of all ages. Try fencing, or learn to dance salsa. Be imaginative. What do you really want to do?

Glossary

apathetic   Disinterested, having no feeling or enthusiasm for anything.

calluses   Areas of hardened skin.

calorie   A unit for measuring the energy value of food.

cholesterol   The substance in animal fats which can contribute to heart disease if consumed in large quantities.

craving   An irresistible urge or desire for something.

dehydration   Lacking water or fluid in your body, which causes many side effects.

emaciated   Extremely thin.

genetic   A characteristic you are born with.

hormones   Chemical substances in the body which perform important functions.

laxatives   Tablets which stop you from digesting food by making you go to the toilet.

metabolic rate   The rate at which your body uses up calories.

nauseous   Feeling sick.

peer pressure   Feeling the need to be like other people of the same age or type.

psychological   Relating to the mind.

puberty   The period of time in your teens when your body changes, as a result of hormones.

self-esteem   A good opinion of oneself.

subliminal   The use of images to influence someone without him or her knowing it.

therapy   A method of understanding and solving problems by talking, guided by a trained specialist.

Further Reading

Dare to be you. A revolutionary handbook for teenage health and good looks by Susannah Kenton (Lightning, 1990)

Adolescence by Elizabeth Fenwick and Tony Smith (Dorling Kindersley, 1993)

Catherine - the story of a young girl who died of anorexia by Maureen Dunbar (Penguin, 1987)

The Anorexic Experience (especially Chapter 7) by Marilyn Lawrence (Women's Press, 1984)

Useful addresses

Eating Disorders Association
Sackville Place
44 Magdalen Street
Norwich
NR3 1JE

Women's Therapy Centre
6 Manor Gardens
London
N7 6LA

They run therapy groups and will send out information and a booklist of further reading.

Raleigh International
Raleigh House
27 Parsons Green Lane
London
SW6 4HZ

Acknowledgements

Thanks to the following organizations which supplied the photographs used in this publication: APM Photographic 6, 9 (bottom); The Bridgeman Art Library 28 (Bather Sitting Drying her Leg, c. 1910 by Pierre Auguste Renoir (1841-1919) Museo de Arte, Sao Paulo Giraudon / Bridgeman Art Library, London; Colorific 20 (Dan Goodrich), 27 (Jean Paul Nacivet); Eye Ubiquitous 5 (bottom, Mostyn), 8 (Skjold), 19 (Steven Rafferty), 21, 43 (Sean Aidan), 44 (Matthew McKee), 45 (Bryan Pickering); Sally and Richard Greenhill 16; Horizon 7 (Daniel Levin); Images Colour Library 42; Popperfoto 40, 41; Reflections Photolibrary 33, 36-7; Rex Features 5 (top), 29 (Today); Science Photo Library 14, 24 (Louise Williams), 25 (BSIP, Seigneury Conseil), 30 (David Gifford), 31 (BSIP); Skjold Picture Library 22 (both), 23, 32, 34, 35, 38-9; Tony Stone Worldwide 4 (Gerard Loucel), 13 (Penny Tweedie), 18 (Penny Tweedie), 26 (Penny Tweedie); The Telegraph Colour Library 9 (top, S. Benbow), 10 (S. Benbow), 10-11 (A.Tilley), 12 (G. Harrison), 15.

Index